T0193521

Other Inspirational books by Joyce A. Boahene:

The Eyes of Perfect Love

https://www.amazon.com/Eyes-Perfect-Love-Joyce-Boahene/ dp/149848834X

Quiet Time Companion http://amzn.to/191K1oR

Devotional Prayer Journal http://amzn.to/1eqPslj

Meditations Of The Heart http://amzn.to/19M2VTJ

Inspirational Poems http://www.amazon.com/gp/aw/d/1598243977

Prayer Partner Journal http://www.amazon.com/gp/aw/d/1598243969

Don't You Quit http://www.amazon.com/gp/aw/d/1598243810

THE POETIC WORD https://www.amazon.com/Poetic-Word-Anthology-Poetry-Soul/dp/16642 90915/ref=mp_s_a_1_1?crid=CFUL6DU5G0TH&keywords=joyce+a+boahene+the+poetic +word&qid=1676895590&sprefix=joyce+a+boahene+the+potic+word%2Caps%2C136&sr=8-1

Website: joyceboahene.com

From Pain To Purpose

Joyce A. Boahene

WESTBOW
PRESS*

A DIVISION OF THOMAS NELSON
& ZONDERVAN

Copyright © 2023 Joyce A. Boahene.

All rights reserved. No part of this book may be used or reproduced by any means, graphic, electronic, or mechanical, including photocopying, recording, taping or by any information storage retrieval system without the written permission of the author except in the case of brief quotations embodied in critical articles and reviews.

WestBow Press books may be ordered through booksellers or by contacting:

WestBow Press
A Division of Thomas Nelson & Zondervan
1663 Liberty Drive
Bloomington, IN 47403
www.westbowpress.com
844-714-3454

Because of the dynamic nature of the Internet, any web addresses or links contained in this book may have changed since publication and may no longer be valid. The views expressed in this work are solely those of the author and do not necessarily reflect the views of the publisher, and the publisher hereby disclaims any responsibility for them.

Any people depicted in stock imagery provided by Getty Images are models, and such images are being used for illustrative purposes only.
Certain stock imagery © Getty Images.

Scriptures are taken from the New King James Version®. Copyright © 1982 by Thomas Nelson.
Used by permission. All rights reserved.

Author photo by Charles Wainwright

ISBN: 978-1-6642-9462-2 (sc)
ISBN: 978-1-6642-9461-5 (e)

Library of Congress Control Number: 2023904500

Print information available on the last page.

WestBow Press rev. date: 03/16/2023

I have risen up from the ashes, and the pain of my past; And I am giving God the praises from the depth of my heart. I have risen up from the ashes of neglect and abuse, to be groomed for God's glory and to be a pure vessel He can use!

Contents

Dedication ix

Introduction xiii

Chapter 1   You Have A Purpose 1

Chapter 2   Fear Not 6

Chapter 3   Dream Big 10

Chapter 4   It Is All Training for Reigning 13

Chapter 5   Life Is a Journey 16

Chapter 6   Run with Endurance 19

Chapter 7   Patience 22

Chapter 8   Spirit, Soul, and Body 25

Chapter 9   Forgiveness Is a Choice 28

Chapter 10 Love Is All Around 31

Chapter 11 G- Is For Gratitude 34

Chapter 12 From Pain to Purpose 37

Bibliography 47

Dedication

This devotional book is dedicated to all of my sisters from every walk of life who are in hot pursuit of becoming all that God has created them to be. We are all women of God's creation. We are all daughters of destiny. We are all sisters in the struggle of life. Yet God has called us to make a positive impact on history. This is not only in what we are doing but what we are saying on a daily basis. Let us endeavor in this next decade to grow together, to encourage one another, to use our gifts and talents to impact our world, and to make it a better place for all of humanity.

Sisters in the Making~

We are true sisters in the making;
New territories we are now taking.
We are true sisters rising above complacency
To become all that God has created us to be.

We are true sisters with a divine destiny
That is far greater than the things
That we can feel and see.

We are true sisters making progress,
For every nation to see
That there is hope for their future,
And there is total victory.

Ephesians 2:10 (NKJV) says, "For we are His workmanship, created in Christ Jesus for good works, which God prepared beforehand that we should walk in them."

Some of life's battles may have crushed you, defined you, and even made you bitter. However, don't let people or negative life experiences tell you how you rate. God has a divine purpose for your life. His plan is far greater than your challenges or your pain. His plan goes above and beyond anything you can imagine or ask Him for. His word says that you are fearfully and wonderfully made. Dare to ask God to reveal His plan for your life. Then trust Him to lead you one step at a time.

Let Psalms 139 speak to your heart today. Let it become your daily declaration.

> O Lord, You have searched me and known me. You know my sitting down and my rising up; You understand my thought afar off. You comprehend my path and my lying down, And are acquainted with all my ways. For there is not a word on my tongue, But behold, O Lord, You know it altogether. You have hedged me behind and before, And laid Your hand upon me. Such knowledge is too wonderful for me; It is high, I cannot attain it. Where can I go from Your Spirit? Or where can I flee from Your presence? If I ascend into heaven, You are there; If I make my bed in hell, behold, You are there. If I take the wings of the morning, And dwell in the uttermost parts of the sea, Even there Your hand shall lead me, And Your right hand shall hold me. If I say, "Surely the darkness shall fall on me," Even the night shall be light about me; Indeed, the darkness shall not hide from You, But the night shines as the day; The darkness and the light are both alike to You. For You formed my inward parts; You covered me in my mother's womb. I will praise You, for I am fearfully and wonderfully made; Marvelous are Your works, And that my soul knows very well. (Psalms 139:1–14 NKJV)

You see, God knows who you are. He is also mindful of all the things that you have been through. He wants to heal your soul. He wants to give you a heavenly perspective about your pain. Yes, He wants you to begin to view every lesson as an opportunity to learn, grow, and become better. You are still breathing because your life matters. It matters to Him! You are also here to be a blessing to your family, friends, and vocation. You are here to use your gifts and talents to make a mark on society. Moreover, while you may never fully understand why certain negative things have happened, you can choose to believe and trust that God is able to transform your pain into purpose. "For out of the ashes new life can grow!" It is time for you to discover your true identity. It is time for you to fulfill your divine destiny!

Introduction

We have all tasted from the bitter waters of life. Unfortunately, we live in a society where we are subject to many forms of abuse, violence, and trauma. I grew up watching my mother endure domestic abuse. In my own life, I have indeed tasted from life's bitter waters many times. My earliest memory of my childhood was marked by great physical, emotional, and sexual abuse. I came from Montserrat in the West Indies to the United States at the age of sixteen. It was a journey that I was not mentally prepared for. I experienced severe culture shock coming from that tiny remote island. During my high school years, I had no friends. I suffered from the daily taunting and bullying of my classmates because I wore hand-me-down clothes and spoke with an accent. I told no one about my experiences because I was desperately trying to fit into a culture where I needed to find acceptance and approval. My spoken words were few. Ironically, I found that I excelled in my English class and had a desire to write down my thoughts and feelings. I also had a caring English teacher who recognized that I had a flair for words and encouraged me to continue to read and write.

The moment of some form of purpose and recognition for me came after graduating from college. People began to read my work and were able to identify with the themes and emotions in my writings. From there, they began to request my poetry for their homes and offices or as gifts for someone who had mentored or inspired them.

Over the years, God has been faithfully transforming my pain into purpose. The emotional pain that I have suffered has somehow propelled me to pen more than 400 hundred works of literary prose and twelve inspirational book titles. These writings include contemporary themes such as friendship, love, marriage, family, raising children, faith and spirituality, emotional healing, recovering from grief and loss, and overcoming life's challenges. Over the past two decades, I have been commissioned by church leaders, business officials, and community members alike to compose poetry for special occasions and public events.

Writing has been a constant in my life. As an entrepreneur, I am now able to use my creative writings to develop products that are inspired by faith, perfected by design, functional, and stylish.

My hope is that this devotional book will help you to understand that your purpose is far greater than all of your pain. May it inspire you not only to discover your true purpose, but to pursue it with a passion. Each chapter challenges you to look beyond your natural limitations and see that the horizon is unlimited. 1 Corinthians 2:9 says this, "Eye has not seen, nor ear heard, nor have entered into the heart of man the things which God has prepared for those who love Him." It is my heartfelt prayer that God would take your ashes from the pain of old and turn them into the finest gold.

~ *Your Purpose* ~

Your purpose is far greater
Than all of your pain,
So look for the sunshine
Through the storm and the rain.

Your purpose is far greater
Than all of your fears,
So trust in the Savior
And cast all your cares.

Your purpose is far greater
Than the giants you have known,
So look to the One
Who still sits on the throne.

Chapter 1

You Have A Purpose

Whether you realize it or not, you were created for a purpose. Your purpose goes beyond the traditional things that we as women have been taught, such as getting married and raising a family. God has created each and every person with a unique, individual life plan. Maybe you are called to be an entrepreneur or a philanthropist. Perhaps you are destined to become a CEO of a Fortune 500 company or the next Mother Theresa. Whatever it may be, your purpose is designed to be both a blessing to you and to society as a whole. In his book *The Purpose-Driven Life*, Pastor Rick Warren states, "You were made by God and for God—and until you understand that, life will never make sense."[1]

Three imperatives follow from this.

First, you have to know God. Coming to God begins with a prayer. John 3:16 (NKJV) says, "For God so loved the world that he gave his only begotten Son, that whoever believes in Him should not perish but have everlasting life." Romans 10:9 says that what you confess with your mouth and believe in your heart will ultimately become your reality. Knowing God begins with believing the biblical account of His Son Jesus Christ and that He is willing to use His power on your behalf.

Second, you have to believe that God has a good, acceptable, and perfect plan for your life. You are God's work of art in the earth.

Third, you have to accept your assignment. Accepting your assignment begins with a decision to discover your purpose and pursue it with a passion. This is the area that trips most people up. Why? Because there are many unspoken fears, past mistakes, and failures that flood our minds on a daily basis. In life, we have all experienced challenges and disappointments that try to derail us. However, failure does not have to be final. Often, great understanding, wisdom, and clarity occur when we are willing to examine our past mistakes and failures, grow in the knowledge of the present, and plan more wisely for the future.

---

[1] Rick Warren, *The Purpose-Driven Life* (Grand Rapids, MI: Zondervan, 2002), 19.

Adversity does have a way of teaching us valuable life lessons. Sometimes, out of the ashes and rubble of our lives, we find our true passions, callings, or destinies. However, living life on purpose is infinitely more rewarding than living it by chance or happenstance. Your greatest struggle in life may be the fight to look beyond your natural limitations and embrace the plan that God has for your life.

It is important for you to know these things.

What moves you? What motivates or drives you?

_____
_____
_____
_____
_____

When do you feel most authentic and fulfilled?

_____
_____
_____
_____
_____

What brings you joy?

_____
_____
_____
_____
_____

Start today by taking inventory of your life.

Question for Reflection

Do you know your purpose?

_____

_____

_____

_____

_____

If not, ask God to reveal His divine purpose for your life.

_____

_____

_____

_____

_____

~Refuse~

Refuse to take counsel from fear and doubt,
But trust in Jehovah
To work everything out.

Refuse to take counsel from fear and doubt,
But start off your day with a hallelujah shout.
Refuse to take counsel from fear and doubt,
For faith, hope, and love
Are what true living is really all about!

Chapter 2

Fear Not

Fear, whether real or imagined, is a threat to discovering one's true identity and purpose. Sometimes we can experience fear from past traumatic experiences. We can also face great fear when we find ourselves in the lion's den for speaking the truth or even doing what is right. Doing what is right in the sight of God is not always popular, but the rewards are great. Daniel was a prophet of God. He chose to honor God's ways and ended up in the lion's den. However, just as Daniel was a man of great integrity and commitment, so must you and I be when we encounter any form of adversity in our lives. Hard times come to all of us. Our true faith is not proven by feeling strong but by what we actually *do* in times of great struggle. When we face fear, we have to intend in our hearts to remain true to ourselves and our beliefs. In the end, we will find favor in the sight of God and humankind.

I love the story of Daniel because he changed an entire nation through his excellent spirit and willingness to stand for the truth. When we stand for what is right, our lives are living proof of our convictions but also of our God. When we find ourselves in the lion's den, we can trust God to deliver us and vindicate us from all wrong. Here is the account of how God delivered Daniel from the king who made a decree for him to be destroyed.

> Then the king arose very early in the morning and went in haste to the den of lions. And when he came to the den, he cried out with a lamenting voice to Daniel. The king spoke, saying to Daniel, "Daniel, servant of the living God, has your God, whom you serve continually, been able to deliver you from the lions?" Then Daniel said to the king, "O king, live forever! My God sent His angel and shut the lions' mouths, so that they have not hurt me, because I was found innocent before Him; and also, O king, I have done no wrong before you." Now the king was exceedingly glad for him, and commanded that they should take Daniel up out of the den. So Daniel was taken up out of the den, and no

injury whatever was found on him, because he believed in his God. (Daniel 6:19–23 NKJV)

If you ever find yourself in a dark place, don't fear and don't worry. Yes, it might be dark in there, but that doesn't mean you are alone. God can reach into that circumstance and turn even your greatest enemies into your greatest advocates. Remember, it is always darkest before the dawn.

Merriam-Webster Dictionary describes *fear* as feeling "frighten[ed]" or "to feel fear in (oneself); to have a reverential awe of…to be afraid of: expect with alarm…to be afraid or apprehensive."[2]

The only fear that we should entertain from the above definition is a healthy respect of who God is. Having this type of reverential fear will cause us to gain knowledge and walk in wisdom. Second Timothy 1:7 (NKJV) says, "For God has not given us a spirit of fear, but of power and of love and of a sound mind." Fear in any form must be resisted for it is contagious, and it will bring torment to the heart and mind. Therefore, let us not be afraid of the things that we see, feel, and hear. For no matter what is going on in our lives, God's Word says we are to fear not.

It will take courage to confront our fears and keep going when we are not feeling our best. It takes even more courage to persevere when we cannot see any end in sight. No matter what happens each day, we wake up believing that the sun will shine again. Faith is in operation every day of our lives. It is a very powerful force, and it has corresponding action. Every day by faith we act on what we believe, good or bad. The God kind of faith is actually the highest form of faith, and it is the one that He rewards the most. This kind of faith will require us to leave our comfort zones and step out on limbs. When we choose this level of faith, we dare to believe, dream big, and do something that has never been done before.

---

[2] *Merriam-Webster.com*, s.v. "fear," accessed February 24, 2023, https://www.merriam-webster.com/dictionary/fear.

It is time to identify the fears that are holding you back.

Question for Reflection

Can you identify your fears?

_____
_____
_____
_____
_____

Ask God to help you to face them with courage and overcome them.

_____
_____
_____
_____
_____

~Nothing Is Impossible~

When somebody tells you
That something cannot be done,
Tell them that nothing is impossible
With the help of God's Son.

When somebody tells you
That something cannot be done,
Tell them that through Jesus,
Every battle has already been won.

When somebody tells you
That something cannot be done,
Just pause and thank God
For how far you have come.

Chapter 3

Dream Big

We have all been lost without direction before, and it is not fun. Sometimes our lives can feel just like that—directionless. The great news is that God in His infinite wisdom and mercy has outfitted all of us with an internal GPS system. Your GPS is the still, small voice inside you. It is your "inner gut" that gives you a warning or suggestion about the direction in which you are headed. If you are at a detour in your life, don't despair. Just remember with your dreams and internal GPS, you are still headed in the right direction.

You have heard the phrase "Go big or go home." Dreams are just that: they are so big that you can't go home. In reality, the ability to dream big activates us and stimulates our most creative, purposeful selves. However, no one can fully prepare us for the process that is involved in fulfilling our dreams. *The Oxford Dictionary* describes *process* as "a series of actions or operations conducing to an end."[3]

As you can see from this definition, process will involve growth. This growth is often a stage of intense labor and pain. It is the place where you have to roll up your sleeves, flex your muscles, and sweat. It is the place where you might face the greatest challenge of your life. It is the place where you feel isolated, misunderstood, and persecuted for what you believe. It is the place where no help is forthcoming and you begin to question the vision and provision. Nevertheless, this is the place where you must choose to *press on!* When you hold fast to your dream in spite of opposition, your passion will compel you to pursue and make your dream a reality.

---

[3] "Process." *Merriam-Webster.com Dictionary*, Merriam-Webster, https://www.merriam-webster.com/dictionary/process. Accessed 28 Feb. 2023.

Question for Reflection

What is your dream?

_____

_____

_____

_____

_____

Ask God to give you a strategy to fulfill it.

_____

_____

_____

_____

_____

~Beyond Your Pain~

Beyond your pain,
There is a bountiful gain.
Beyond your disappointments,
God has a new appointment.

Beyond your deepest struggles,
There is a double blessing for your troubles.
Beyond your tears,
There is great faith for your fears.
And beyond man's rejection,
There is God's unconditional love and perfection.

Chapter 4

It Is All Training for Reigning

No matter what you are going through, just remember it's all "training for reigning." *You are a queen.* In case no one has ever told you, you are part of a royal priesthood. There is a scripture in the Bible that says

> But you are a chosen generation, a royal priesthood, a holy nation, His own special people, that you may proclaim the praises of Him who called you out of darkness into His marvelous light." (1 Peter 2:9 NKJV)

There are certain characteristics of a queen. She represents the kingdom that she is part of. She is a woman of noble character. She is loyal and disciplined. She follows protocol. Her outward character is a reflection of her inner beauty. Her words carry weight. She commands respect. She is humble and not prideful. She uses her position to influence or improve the quality of life for her family and the good of society. She is an example for others to follow.

Acting like a queen requires that you change your mindset of how you see yourself. You are not a *victim.* You are an original. You are so unique that God only made one of you. That means that no one else on this earth can walk in the path that has been chosen for you. Not even identical twins have the same fingerprints, handprints, and footprints. Your design by God was intentional. Therefore, you have to be determined to live your life intentionally. This will require you to take inventory of your thoughts, what you say about yourself, and above all the actions that you take on a regular basis. What you think and constantly speak will set the course and direction of your life.

Life is too precious to waste trying to be something that others want you to be .You are a genuine gem, and there is only *one of you*! It is time to break off the limitations that others have placed on you. More importantly, you must take off the limitations that you have placed on yourself. Let your joy and peace spring forth from knowing that you were created for a purpose. You are valuable to God and you are an asset to your family and friends.

Keep on shining wherever you go, and you will reap a great harvest in the lives that you sow. Keep on shining for you are a gift to the world. Remember to live by the conviction that is deep in your soul.

Question for Reflection:

Who and what are you allowing to define you?

_____

_____

_____

_____

_____

Let God's word define who you are. Find scriptures that tell you who you are in Christ.

_____

_____

_____

_____

_____

~Life's Journey~

If it had not been for your good grace,
Dear Lord, where would I be?
If it had not been for your good grace,
Life's journey would have been
A very painful race.

Lord, if it had not been for your good grace,
I would have no courage to endure
And keep up with the pace.

Lord, if it had not been for your good grace,
My soul would have been permanently trapped
In a very awful place.

Chapter 5

Life Is a Journey

Life is a journey that we all have to take. Successful navigation is dependent on the quality decisions that we make from day to day.

The steps on this journey are as follows.

(1) Know God's plan for your life
When we don't know God's plan, other people will make plans for us that fit into their schedules.

(2) Write it down
Write down what you are passionate about. The Bible says to write the vision and make it plain.

> Then the LORD answered me and said: "Write the vision And make it plain on tablets, That he may run who reads it. For the vision is yet for an appointed time; But at the end it will speak, and it will not lie. Though it tarries, wait for it; Because it will surely come, It will not tarry." (Habakkuk 2:2–3 NKJV)

Writing down your own personal vision means getting your ideas from your head onto paper. This can also help to reaffirm your true purpose and give you focus.

(3) Make preparation
That would mean preparing yourself naturally, spiritually, physically, emotionally, academically, and financially.

(4) Take action
That would mean taking responsibility for your life, not procrastinating, and instead doing.

~ It is never too late to learn a new skill.
~ Go ahead and take some classes.
~ Access knowledge (through self-help books, websites, and so on)
~ Seek out a mentor in the area of interest you want to pursue.
~ Above all, don't forget to ask God to give you direction and success.

There will always be light on the pathway of life if we humbly seek God for wisdom for everyday living. Here is a promise from Psalm 119:105 that you can believe and confess daily. "Your word is a lamp to my feet, And a light to my path."

Question for Reflection:

Do you know where you are going?

_____

_____

_____

_____

_____

Ask God to be your navigator.

_____

_____

_____

_____

_____

~Endurance~

May God open your eyes
To see that much higher call;
And may you run with endurance
As you give Him your all.

May God open your ears
To hear the voice of the King;
And may He receive the sacrifice of worship
And the true honor that you bring.

May God open your heart
To the joy that's within;
And may He help you to give thanks
For He is doing a new thing.

Chapter 6

Run with Endurance

Merriam-Webster Dictionary defines *grace* as "unmerited divine assistance given [to] humans for their regeneration or sanctification."[4] Similarly, it defines a *race* as "a set course…or a duration of time"[5] or the course of life. Every person on this earth has a set course or "race" for his or her life as ordained by God. We can be certain that along our paths, Heaven is continually sending us divine assistance.

As with any race, the distance may be long and the terrain physically taxing. Professional athletes know they can optimize their race-day performance by reducing excess weight, building endurance, and practicing enhanced focus.

We too, can optimize our life "race" by practicing the same skills. Hebrews 12, verses 1-2 urges us to "lay aside every weight, and the sin which so easily ensnares us, and let us run with endurance the race that is set before us, looking unto Jesus, the author and finisher of our faith."

Consider these three areas concerning optimal life performance.

1. Weights are things that slow us down. They may be bad habits, certain mindsets, behaviors, attitudes, or unnecessary stress and anxiety. Take inventory of the things that slow you down and make a concerted effort to lay aside negative behaviors.
2. Endurance is built over time and through experience. Life brings many events and sometimes challenges that serve to increase our endurance. The changes experienced coupled with God's grace work together to strengthen us. 2 Corinthians 12:9 says this, "My grace is sufficient for you, for my strength is made perfect in weakness."

---

[4] *Merriam-Webster.com*, s.v. "grace," accessed February 24, 2023, https://www.merriam-webster.com/dictionary/grace.

[5] *Merriam-Webster.com*, s.v. "race," accessed February 24, 2023, https://www.merriam-webster.com/dictionary/race.

3. Envision the end results of the race that you are running. Consider the end of your set life course. What will you have accomplished? What would Jesus say about your race? When the race gets tough, focus instead on the end result. Proverbs 14:23 says that you can take comfort in knowing that, "In all labor there is profit."

Question for Reflection

Whose race are you running?

_____

_____

_____

_____

_____

Ask God to set and maintain your pace.

_____

_____

_____

_____

_____

~Exercise Patience~

Keep planting seeds of goodness
Wherever you go,
And you will surely reap a great harvest before you know.
Start out daily with love for everyone,
And never count the scores for the wrongs they have done.

Always share an element of joy,
And never seek to slander, hurt, or destroy.
Offer up peace instead of war,
In the midst of life's conflicts and uproar.
Exercise patience through the storm,
And allow God to lead you daily
With His outstretched arms.

Chapter 7

Patience

Patience really is a virtue. It is, "the capacity, habit, or fact of being patient."[6] Exercising that kind of patience requires adopting a lifestyle of positive perseverance. However, in our modern age and way of thinking, we often equate patience with waiting or a lack of productivity.

Contrary to what we believe, patience is not an impotent state, but a time when we are pregnant with potential. During the waiting season of our lives, there is a work that is being performed in and upon us. So often, this is the stage that we want to bypass. Yet this is the very place where our greatest growth and development is taking *shape*. In this place, there is an opportunity for quiet reflection, meditation, evaluation and self-regulation.

The waiting period is a time when we might feel like our lives are in holding patterns. However, it is also a time when we are compelled to take inventory and ask ourselves what really matters. As we do, we are able to reorder our priorities and make the necessary changes that will help us to move forward and make progress. There is strength in waiting. Isaiah 40:31 says, "But those who wait on the LORD Shall renew their strength; They shall mount up with wings like eagles, They shall run and not be weary, They shall walk and not faint." Every time we exercise patience, we will grow a bit steadier on our life journeys. That is something we can all be thankful for.

---

[6] "Patience." *Merriam-Webster.com Dictionary*, Merriam-Webster, https://www.merriam-webster.com/dictionary/patience. Accessed 28 Feb. 2023.

Question for Reflection

Are you willing to submit to the process for spiritual growth and maturity?

_____

_____

_____

_____

_____

Ask God to help you to daily develop patience and make progress towards spiritual maturity.

_____

_____

_____

_____

_____

~Take Time~

Take time to relax
And take control.
Take time to be kind
To your body and soul.

Take time to give thanks
For the air that you breathe.
Take time to give thanks
For God has all that you need.

Chapter 8

Spirit, Soul, and Body

You are more than just a physical body. You have an inner core that is called the spirit. Your spirit is that inner part of you that no one else but God can see. It is that unique part of you that connects you to God and allows you to communicate with Him in prayer. The inner core of your spirit is the real *you*. Your spirit is really the true engine that causes life to continually flow within your physical body. Without the life of the spirit, there is *no breath*. The soul is the mind, emotion, and will. This is the command center where we make the decisions that pertain to everyday living. This is the place where the battles of life are either won or lost. Often your head will contradict your heart. This internal tug-of-war can inevitably leave us feeling as though we are double-minded, which is not pretty.

The fact is that you might have a conviction in your heart but still struggle with thoughts of fear and doubt in your head. It happens to all of us. Nevertheless, you cannot allow yourself to permanently park in that place. You have to discipline your mind to line up with the word of God. For James 1:8 very clearly states that, "a double minded man is unstable in all of his ways."

If you are doing all that you know to do and you are still feeling tired and discouraged, it is probably a sign that you need a break from the everyday routine. So often in our hurried pace of life, we do not get many opportunities to rest, relax, and be still. As a result, our lives can begin to feel like whirlwinds. At times like this, it is best to find a place where you can pamper your physical body and also take time to nurture your soul. In that place of solitude, you will find an opportunity for prayer, reading, meditation, and journaling.

Journaling is one of the most effective ways to pour out what is on your heart without fear or inhibition. It is a great way to unload from the burdens of life and cares of the day. Above all, it can help you to write the vision for your life and chart the progress. When you journal, you can be completely honest about what you are feeling. In the process, you can begin to identify and appreciate the little as well as the big things that you can be thankful for. As you allow those things to become your center of focus, you will develop an attitude of gratitude. When you choose to be grateful, your perspective of your natural circumstances will suddenly begin to shift. You will become more aware of the visible signs of God's goodness, which will cause your heart to become more open, more loving, more grateful, and more self-aware. Everybody needs a daily spiritual practice, and journaling truly provides a window for looking into your soul.

Thus, the goal is simple: aim to become single-minded. How might you do that? Well, one key is to let your heart persuade your head. Do this by confessing with your mouth what you believe in your heart and allow yourself to be persuaded that God will deliver on His promises.

Learn how to meditate on God's word with reflection and recitation along your path to single-mindedness:

Question for Reflection

How are you spending your life? Where are you keeping your focus?

_____

_____

_____

_____

_____

Write down some things that you can do daily to nurture your spirit, soul, and body.

_____

_____

_____

_____

_____

~Always Forgive~

Thank God for the angelic host
And the power of the Holy Ghost.
Thank God for His unfailing love
And His mercy shown from heaven above.

Thank God that you are forgiven
And you can always forgive;
For Jesus has provided the first example
Of how you should live.

Chapter 9

Forgiveness Is a Choice

No one ever said that life would be easy. Whether our pain has come from the hand of others or by our own foolish mistakes, we still need the gift of forgiveness.

At times, it may feel difficult to forgive someone depending upon the wrong that person has done to us. It may seem even harder to forgive ourselves for our own failures and shortcomings. The most beautiful story of forgiveness that I have ever heard of is about Peter. Jesus, in His dealings with Peter, demonstrated that forgiveness is a choice and not a feeling. Jesus provided an example of love and forgiveness to a man who denied Him not once but three times.

As a result of receiving forgiveness, Peter was restored to fellowship and was able to continue in service to the Lord. In the book of Acts 2, that same Peter stood up on the day of Pentecost and preached a powerful sermon that impacted the lives of many people.

The same love and forgiveness that was available to Peter is also available to us when we miss the mark. God expects us to always receive forgiveness and extend that same mercy to others. When we receive forgiveness, it releases us from bondage to fear, guilt, shame, and condemnation. Forgiving others releases them from a life of wrath and judgment. John 20:23 (NKJV) says," If you forgive the sins of any, they are forgiven them; if you retain the sins of any, they are retained."

Pause today and take a quick inventory of your life. As you do, ask God to help you to release anyone, including yourself, from unforgiveness. Holding bitterness and unforgiveness is not a healthy way for anyone to live. Love and forgiveness are two pearls that we can always choose to give daily.

Question for Reflection

Are you still holding a grudge?

_____

_____

_____

_____

_____

If you are, it is time to forgive.

_____

_____

_____

_____

_____

~God's Love~

God's love is the voice
That speaks peace and calm.
His love is the anchor
That keeps you holding on.

God's love will pick you up
When you are feeling down.
His love will calm the storm
And turn things around.

God's love will spread the table
With your daily bread;
His love will give you courage
For the journey that's ahead.

Chapter 10

Love Is All Around

When you think about it, the human capacity to love is amazing. Love is actually all around us. Yes, we were created to love and be loved. However the impact of physical, sexual, verbal, and emotional abuse can lead to feelings of anxiety, fear, and even depression.

Often abuse can leave us feeling like we are damaged goods. For many, love is something to be feared rather than embraced. Whether we have experienced the touch and nurturing of human love, we can be confident that God first loved us. God's love is by far the greatest force that we can encounter in this life. Romans 8: 35 (NKJV) asks the question, "Who shall separate us from the love of Christ?"

God's love is perfect and it is not based upon our performance or good works. This love is more difficult to grasp if you have come from a background of abuse. Webster's dictionary describes *abuse* as "corrupt practice or custom…improper or excessive use or treatment."[7] If you have experienced an abusive parent, your first impression of God would be that of an authoritarian rather than a loving Father. If so, you might be struggling to accept His help in working through your past physical or emotional pain.

Your abuser may never tell you that he or she is sorry. Even if the person did, the person can never repay you for the pain that was inflicted upon you. Your Creator is the only one who can heal your soul and remove the memory of your past. A meaningful life can only begin when you choose to believe and receive the gift of His love. God's love, which is perfect, cannot be earned. Ignorance of God's love can keep you in bondage to fear and life circumstances (self-loathing). It is never too late to take back your power from your abuser. Start today by reaching out to God, supportive family, and your community resources.

---

[7] *Merriam-Webster.com,* s.v. "abuse," accessed February 24, 2023, https://www.merriam-webster.com/dictionary/abuse.

Question for Reflection

Are you playing the victim or walking as a victor?

_____

_____

_____

_____

_____

Open up your heart to God's love and beauty that daily surrounds you. What do you see?

_____

_____

_____

_____

_____

~Give Thanks~

If you have breath in your lungs
And a place to lie down,
You still have a good reason
To pause and give thanks.

If you have food on the table
And a few dollars in the bank
It is more than enough
To pause and give thanks.

If you have clothes on your back
And you know that God is your rock,
That is more than enough
To stay on the right track.

Chapter 11

G- Is For Gratitude

Not everything that happens in life can be called good. However, God has the power to transform us in the painful process and work out everything together for His purpose and our good. Romans 8:28 says, "And we know that all things work together for good to those who love God, to those who are called according to His purpose." The key is that we must love God, commit to His will, and trust Him even when things do not make any sense to our natural minds.

An attitude of thanksgiving is an effective way of dealing with the unanswered questions and disappointments in life. It is also a way of magnifying God above the circumstances.

Laughter and joy are also the best medicine. They go a long way to improving our outlooks and moods, which has beneficial effects on our health.

The great thing about joy is that:

- It is contagious;
- It does not cost you anything; and
- It is available 24/7.

The best news is that there are no side effects. Today, choose to laugh and become a bearer of joy. Remember to spread it lavishly wherever you go.

As you walk through this season of your life, I would encourage you to write down at least one thing that you are thankful for. Let that one thing become your focus of attention and joy. Open your mouth and thank God for the one thing that you have identified. As you do, He will break through the darkness and flood your heart with His joy and peace.

Question for Reflection

Are you fretting or praying?

_____

_____

_____

_____

_____

Go ahead and start an honest conversation with God. He is all ears.

_____

_____

_____

_____

_____

~Weep No More~

Weep no more
For the things you have lost,
But lay your pain and disappointments
At the foot of the Cross.

Weep no more
For the wasted years,
But embrace the bright future
That I have prepared.

Weep no more
For the things that are dead,
But let my power and my glory resurrect you instead.

Weep no more
For I have delivered your soul
And my ordained plans for your future
I will surely unfold.

Chapter 12

From Pain to Purpose

In the midst of the greatest technological age, people seem to be under tremendous pressure. Like never before, we are faced with increasing threats of terrorism, wars, rumor of wars, earthquakes, flood warnings, healthcare crises, and the ongoing economic crisis. As if these issues are not enough, we are also faced with our own personal barrenness and pain that is reflected in the ashes of our past.

Many have lost hope and can see no way out. Yet God has promised to take our pain and transform it into purpose when we put our trust in Him. When we look to Him for wisdom and direction, our personal pain can give way to new or renewed purpose and hope.

Developing positive perseverance is a key to continual personal growth and advancement. In life, we can learn how to develop patience and make progress towards perfection or maturity. We are all works in progress. We are under construction by God, who is the master architect and general contractor. Every day that we wake up brings us that much closer to perfection. Philippians 1:6 indicates that God is committed to complete what He has started in you and me.

Today is a different day than yesterday and tomorrow. Each twenty-four-hour day unfolds a unique set of circumstances that we can consider temporary because they are subject to change with the passage of time. If our circumstances are subject to change, then we can choose to not let our temporary "problems" make us bitter. We can shift our focus to becoming better people by maintaining a positive attitude; this is an important key to personal victory. Murmuring and complaining about current circumstances robs us of our joy, prolongs our suffering, and causes needless pain for the people we love.

You must stop beating yourself up about your shortcomings or failures. Admit that you are not perfect but a work in progress. Acknowledge and embrace the work that God is doing in you. Reach out and allow His love and mercy to penetrate every fiber of your being. Follow His work orders. He has a master plan for your life, one that only He can reveal and fulfill. Your part is to simply accept the plan and follow it. Be grateful for the little things in your life. Thank God for continually working on you and showing you His patience. Relax and rest in the knowledge that God in His faithfulness will supply everything that you need to fulfill your destiny. Take joy in knowing that you are still under construction. Your race may have started with a tumultuous beginning but you will end up with a victorious finish. Make a quality decision to run your God-given race and become an instrument of change.

Question for Reflection

Will you trust God to finish the work that He has started in you?

_____
_____
_____
_____
_____

If you are a believer in Christ, God is committed to grace you for the race that He has called you to run. So commit your days, ways, and works unto Him. Then let him instruct you daily how, when, and where to invest your time, energy, finances, and gifts.

God has promised restoration for everything that you have lost. Joel 2:25–26 NKJV says this: "You shall eat in plenty and be satisfied, and praise the name of the LORD your God, Who has dealt wondrously with you; And My people shall never be put to shame."

If you do not have a personal relationship with Jesus Christ, why not start off this new decade by surrendering your life to Him? Romans 10, verses 9-10 guarantees, "That if you confess with your mouth the Lord Jesus and believe in your heart that God has raised Him from the dead, you will be saved. For with the heart one believes unto righteousness, and with the mouth confession is made unto salvation."

When you take this first step of faith, God will gather up the fragments from your life and begin the process of transforming your pain into purpose.

~Let God~

Let God take the ashes,
From the pain of old
And turn them into the finest gold.

Let God take the ashes,
From the pain and abuse
And groom you to be a golden vessel,
That will bear much fruits.

Let God take the ashes,
From the years of rejection
And show you His perfect love,
And divine protection

Notes

Notes

Notes

Notes

Notes

Notes

Bibliography

Warren, Rick. *The Purpose-Driven Life*. Grand Rapids, MI: Zondervan, 2002.

Printed in the United States
by Baker & Taylor Publisher Services